LIT ASF
COLORING BOOK

© Published in 2021.

No part of this production may be reproduced, stored in a retrieval system, or transmitted in any form or by any means, electronic, mechanical, photocopying, recording, or otherwise, without the prior permission of the publishers.

THIS COLORING BOOK BELONGS TO:

_____

_____

WAYS TO WEED

ACROSS
2. is the most recognized cannabinoid in the marijuana plant, delivers a lighter, cleaner high
4. one of the three classifications of cannabis, this plant is less common than the other two
5. marijuana-infused products that are consumed orally, versus smoking flower or concentrate
7. portable and typically uses pre-filled cartridges
8. is a store that legally sells marijuana in a variety of forms, as well as other products, including paraphernalia and clothing
9. a very thick blunt or joint containing a large amount of marijuana
14. a joint or blunt of marijuana that was prepared before its intended time of consumption
15. the part of a smoking apparatus where the marijuana flower is loaded
16. is usually a glass, ceramic, or plastic apparatus that is used to smoke cannabis flowers, herbal extracts, or tobacco.
17. one of the three classifications of cannabis, which offers the user a very relaxing body high

DOWN
1. used to intentionally change one's state of consciousness in order to produce feelings of elation
3. cannabidiol is one of over 60 molecules called cannabinoids found in the marijuana plant
5. term in reference to the use of cannabis to treat chronic pain, nausea, anxiety, sleep apnea & more
10. any type of cannabis product, including lotions, balms or creams that are applied to the outside of a user's body to help with medicinal issues
11. is a rolled cigarette filled with marijuana
12. is created by dumping out the tobacco of a store-bought cigar then rerolling the cigar with marijuana.
13. one of the three classifications of cannabis, well known for its energetic and uplifting cerebral effects, often to treat depression and encourage creativity and amiability

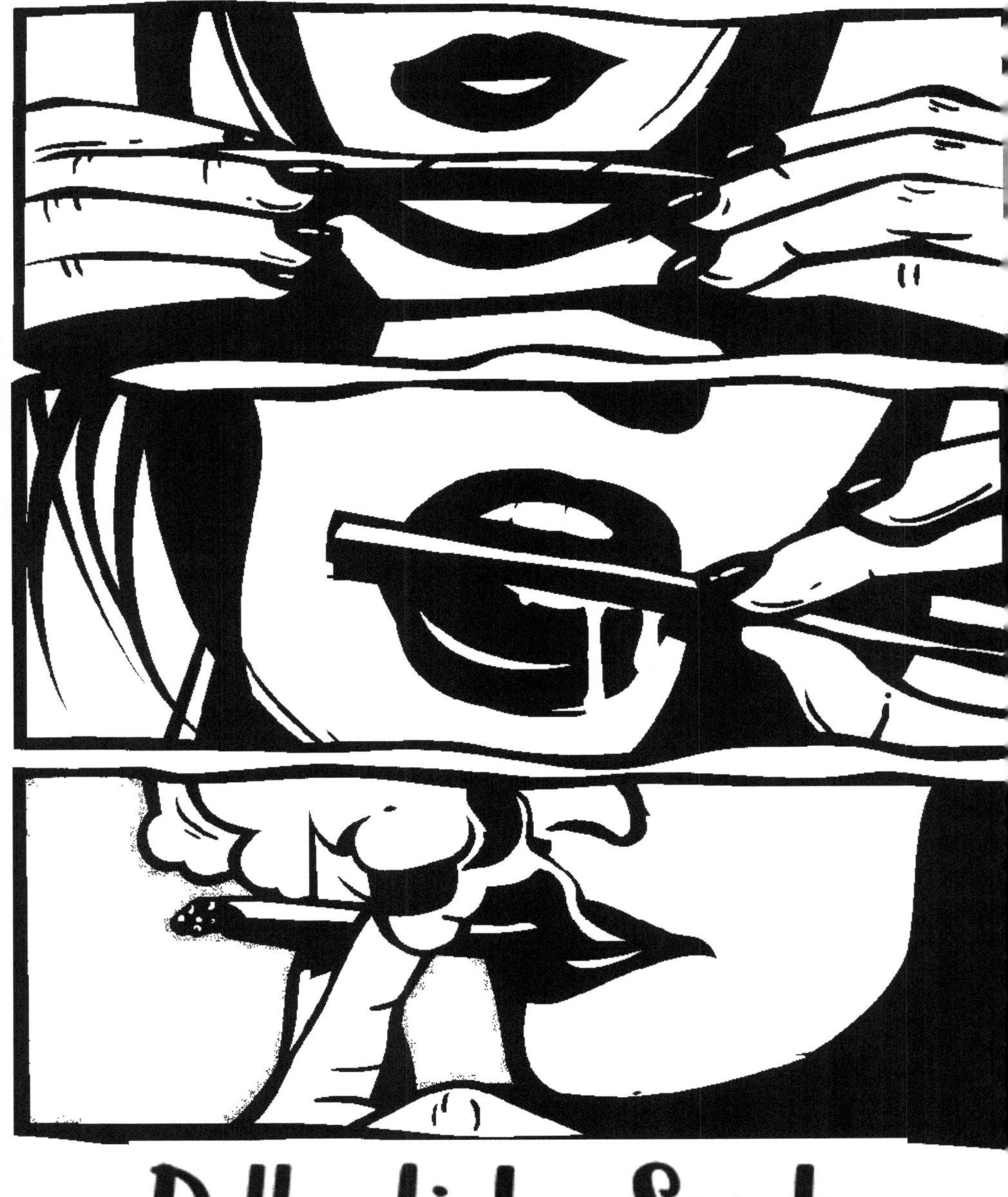

Munchie Maze

SMOKING HELPED PUT ME IN TOUCH WITH THE REALM OF THE SENSES

YES WE SMOKE OVER HERE

```
L R G E T T D D M I N G S A S
E L E I T R U O A H A A V N I
S I N F U G O P R A T F I A B
E T S G E S L E Y I D J K U A
I L Y R H E M P V S O U R J N
D G E S U H R A J V N D B I N
T A X A G J S M O K E G A R A
K S Y P F Y A Y Z E X J L A C
H H O H S A H N W T N A O M I
E T V S Y I N R E A C F S R Y
R E A A P E N Z G I K N U K S
B R N Z L P K Q D J M Q G D C
G K T B I L O E P U R P A O J
G X S S S R M R Z N H V M C S
U R H M K U S H S H F P M H A
```

bud	cannabis	diesel	kush	leaf	loud
dope	drug	ganja	marijuana	mary	medical
gas	grass	hash	pot	purp	reefer
hemp	herb	jane	Sativa	skunk	smoke
			sour	weed	

_____ & _____

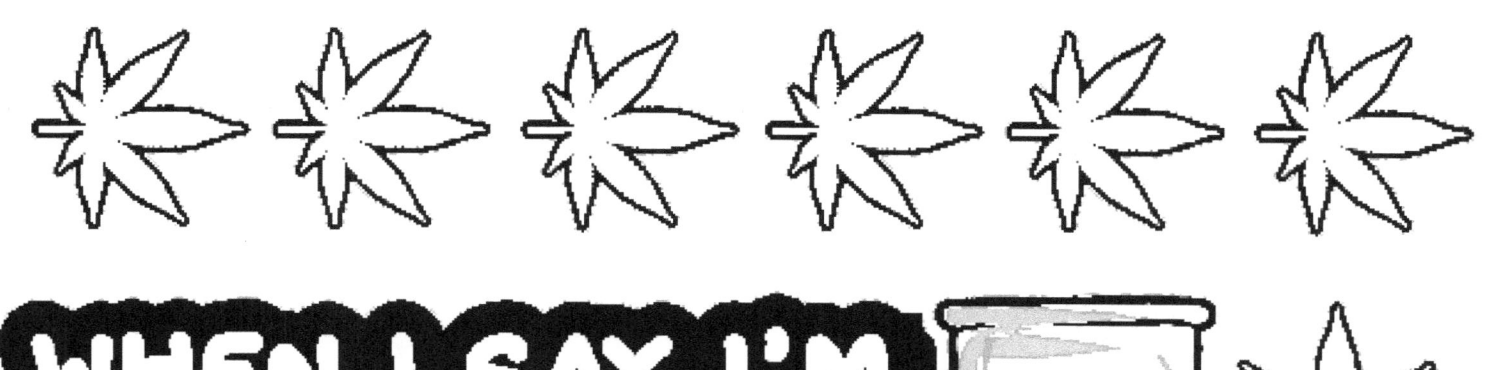

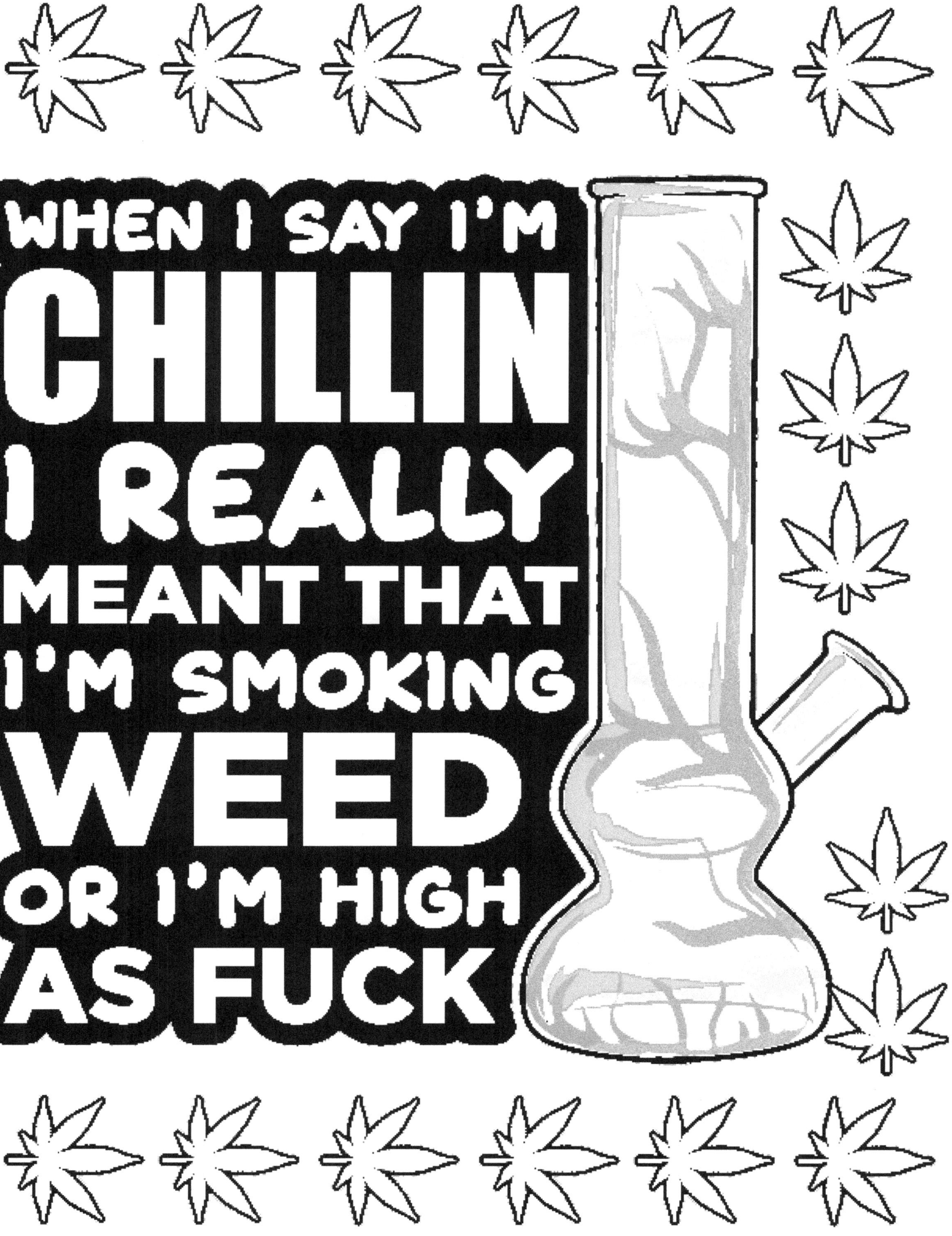
WHEN I SAY I'M
CHILLIN
I REALLY
MEANT THAT
I'M SMOKING
WEED
OR I'M HIGH
AS FUCK

WHEN GETTING HIGH

```
E F S H D S W J W T H L G E C
R P U O N K G U M E I M R N O
B E O U Y C O D M G E E I I T
N F T D K A B H H K D D N Z T
O K C A J N R T P E Z B D A O
I T V D W S E T L B L V E G N
D N O R F R H A G K J Z R A M
P G W B C H C Q P N S T M M O
C A S T A S H B O X I U D Y U
B G P T U O M Q J H N L E C T
K I L E L H O K H C R C L Q H
E X H W R D S P H N D R O O D
Y A R T H S A I L A B O S H R
Q Y O H K Q E X X Q F H E Z L
Y X B I J W S J N S M X O R D X
```

Ashtray CottonMouth Food
Grinder Gum Lighter
Magazine Munchies Papers
RollingTray Scale Snacks
StashBox Water Weed

SUDOKU

3					6	7	4	
1	7	4	3	9		6		
9	6			7	4	3	5	1
7							6	
6	9	1		3				
2	4		6	5	1	9		
		9			7		3	
			5		9	8		6
5		6	4	8	3	2		7

Weed Cinema

Match the movie title with correct actors

MOVIE TITLE

1. ☐ HOW HIGH
2. ☐ BEACH BUM
3. ☐ JAY & SILENT BOB
4. ☐ WE'RE THE MILLERS
5. ☐ FRIDAY
6. ☐ HALF BAKED
7. ☐ CHEECH & CHONG
8. ☐ PINEAPPLE EXPRESS
9. ☐ HIGH SCHOOL
10. ☐ GROW HOUSE
11. ☐ THE WASH
12. ☐ ALI G IN DA HOUSE
13. ☐ THIS IS THE END
14. ☐ HAROLD & KUMAR
15. ☐ THE BIG LEBOWSKI
16. ☐ THE GENTLEMEN
17. ☐ DUDE, WHERE'S MY CAR
18. ☐ BILL & TED'S EXCELLENT ADVENTURE

ACTORS

A. Jennifer Aniston & Jason Sudeikis
B. Tommy & Mr. Marin
C. DeRay Davis & Lil Duval
D. Adrien Brody & Matt Bush
E. John Cho & Kal Penn
F. Sacha Baron Cohen & Emilio Rivera
G. Matthew McConaughey & Charlie Hunnam
H. Dave Chapelle & Jim Breue
I. Method Man & Redman
J. Jeff Bridges & John Goodman
K. Matthew McConaughey & Isla Fisher
L. Ashton Kutcher & Seann William Scott
M. Jason Mewes & Kevin Smith
N. Seth Rogers & James Franco
O. Alex Winter & Keanu Reeves
P. Ice Cube & Chris Tucker
Q. Seth Rogers & Jonah Hill
R. Dr. Dre & Snoop Dogg

WHAT DOES YOUR 420 PLAYLIST LOOK LIKE

We go through different positive and negative emotions when we smoke. Here's a starter playlist of some of my favorites.

Fill the remaining boxes with your favorite songs.

Because I Got High
:Afroman

james Joint
:Rihanna

How High
:Method Man & Redman

Broccoli
:DRAM ft. Lil Yachty

Young, Wild & Free
:Wiz Khalifa & Snoop

Addicted
:Amy Winehouse

We Be Burning
:Sean Paul

Marijuna
:Kid Cudi

The Next Episode
:Dr. Dre & Snoop

Pass The Kouchie
:The Mighty Diamonds

I Got 5 On It
:The Luniz

Hits From The Bong
:Cypress Hill

Stay High
:36Mafia

Mary Jane
:Rick James

Highest In The Room
:Travis Scott

Don't Kill My High
:Lost King

Smoke Break
:Chance Tha Rapper

Blueberry Yum Yum
:Ludacris

Juke Jam
:Chance Tha Rapper

Sativa
:Jhene Aiko

HIGH NOTES ARE IMPORTANT

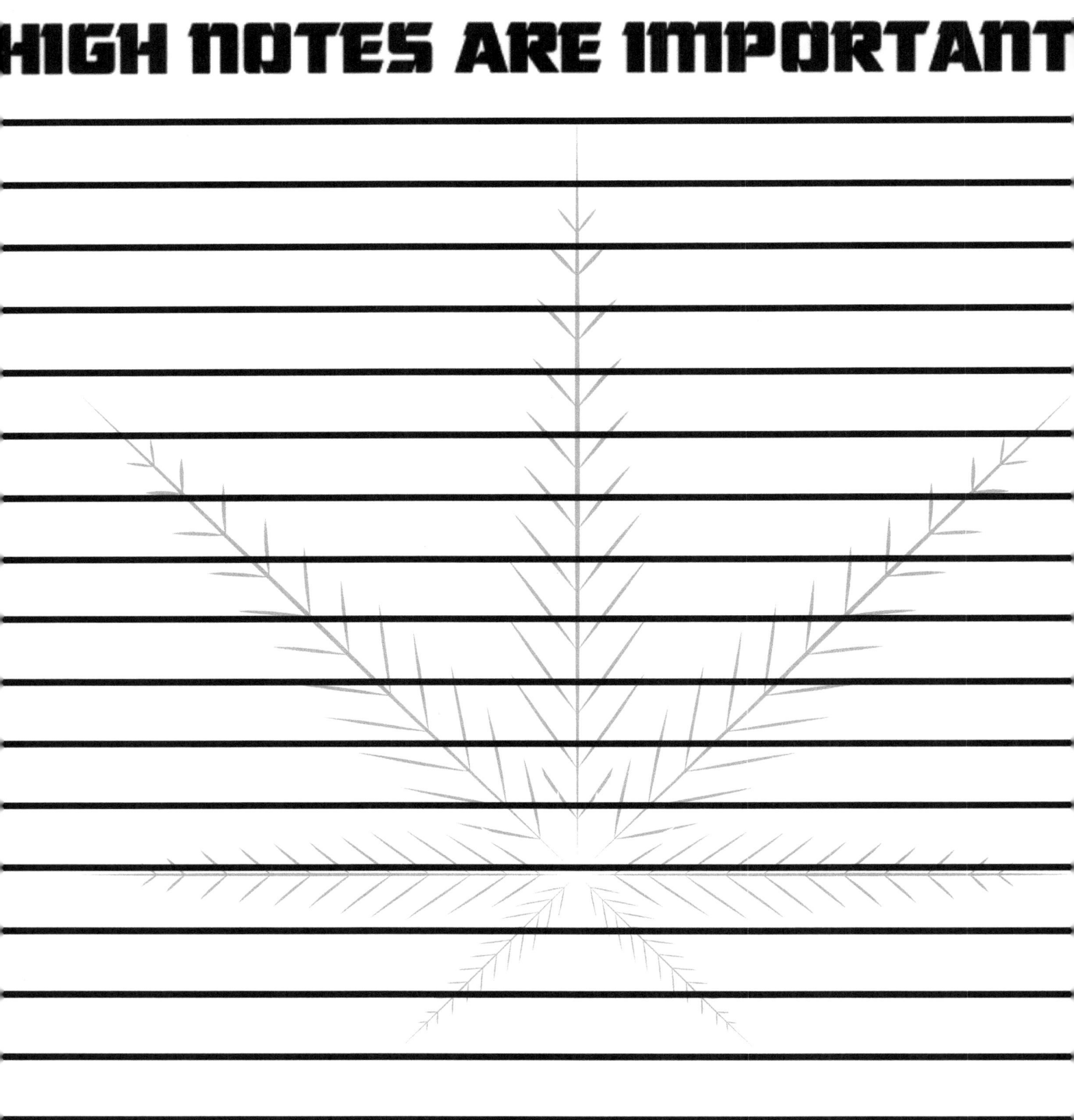

LIT ASF
COLORING BOOK

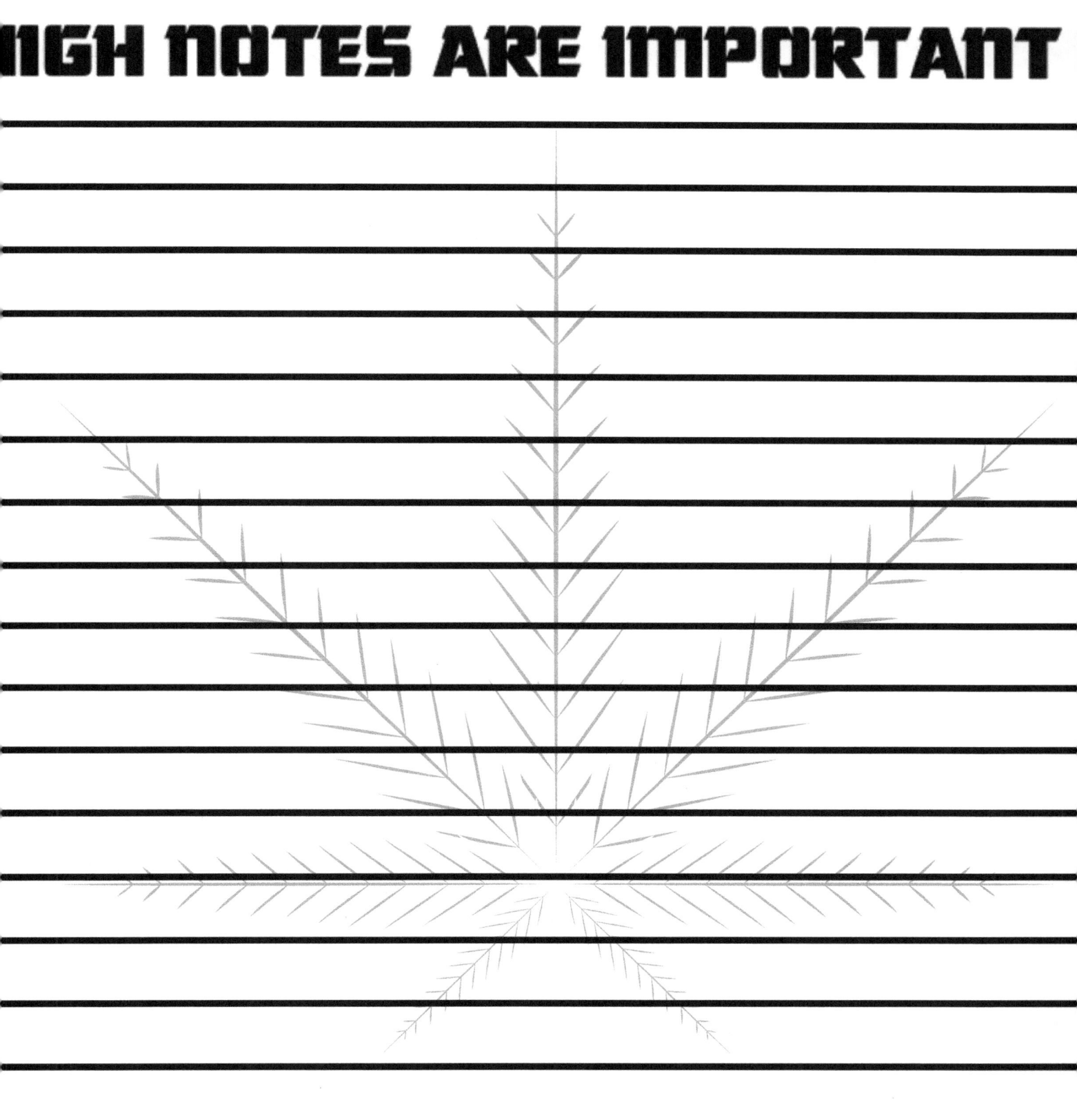

HIGH NOTES ARE IMPORTANT

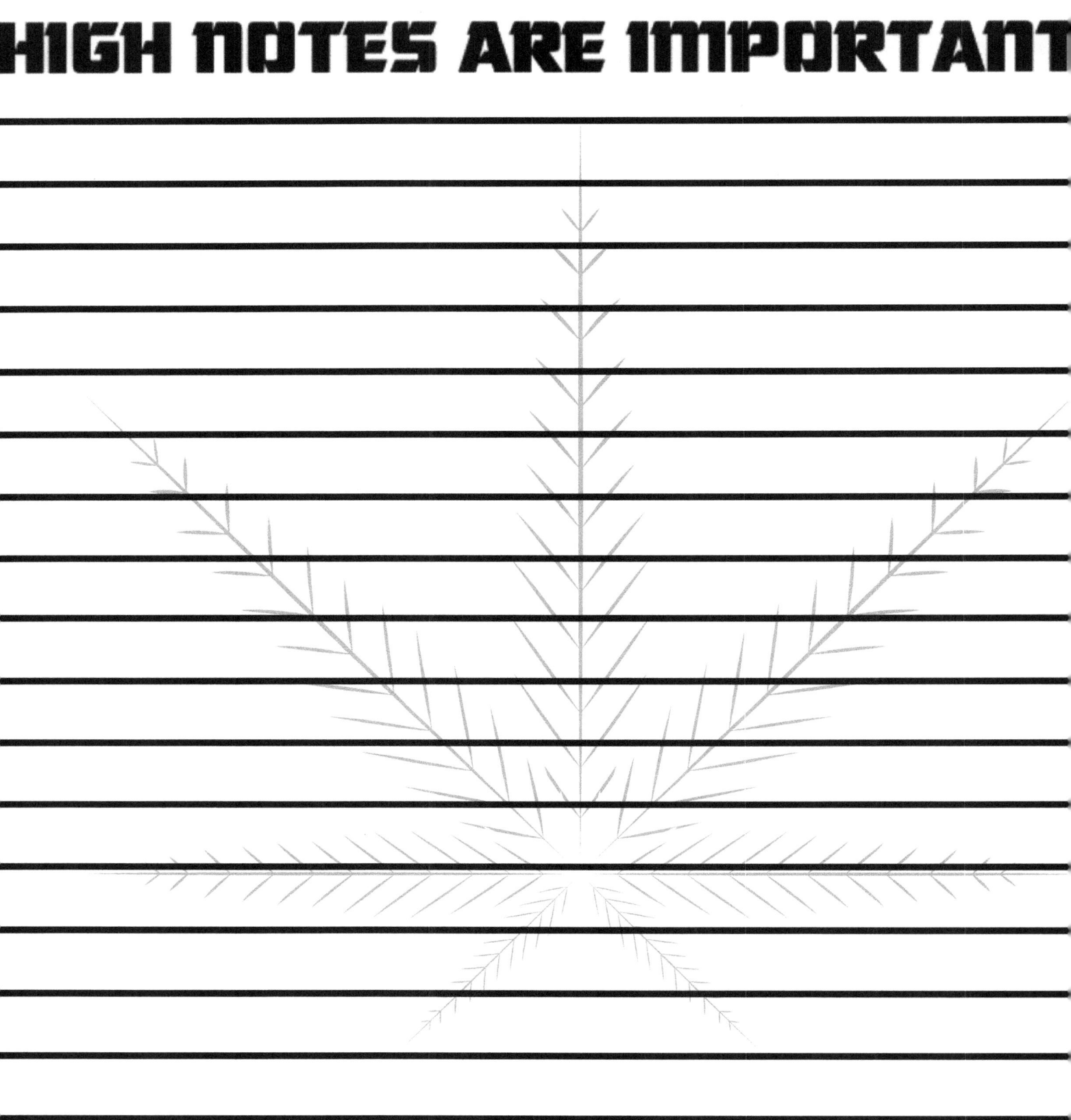

LIT ASF
COLORING BOOK

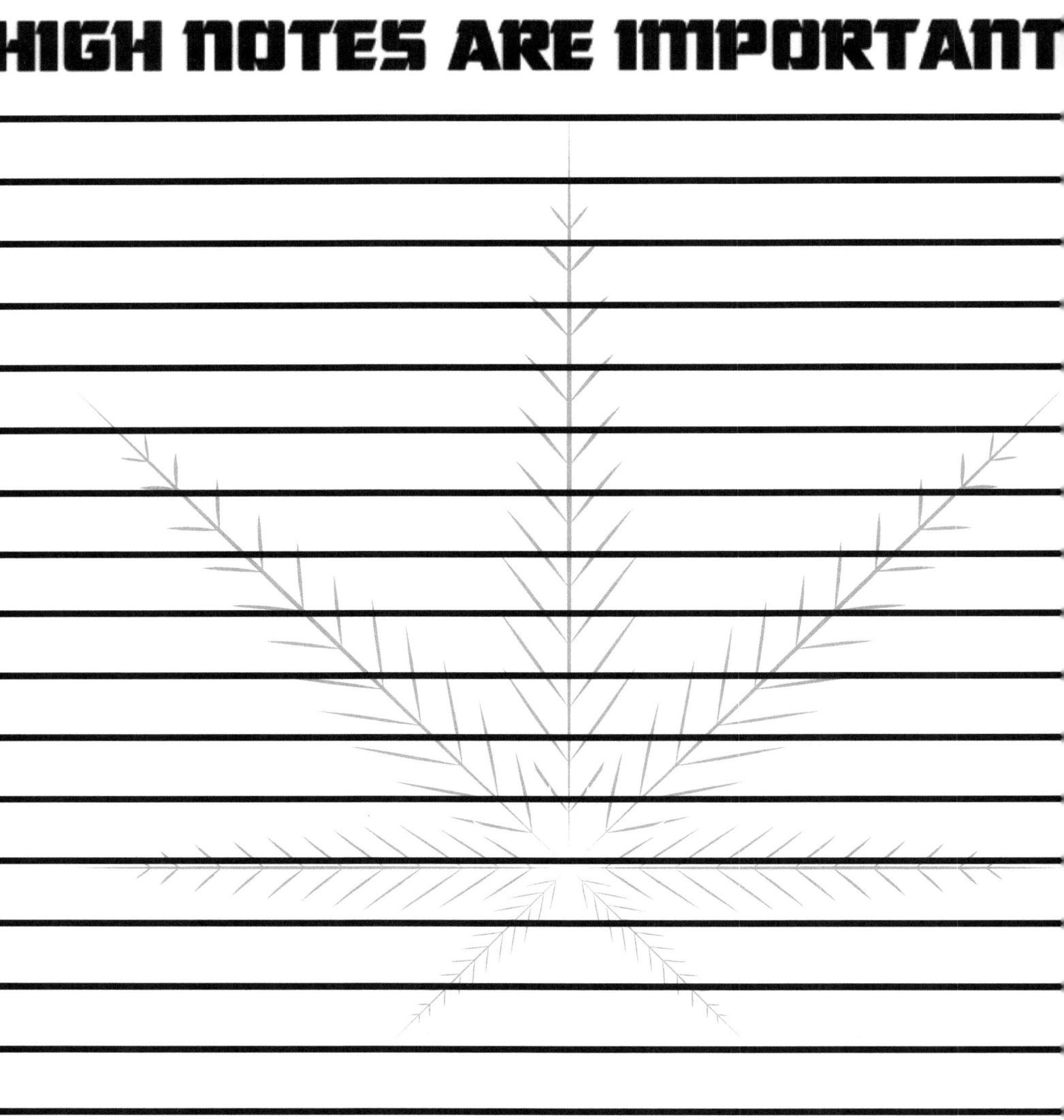

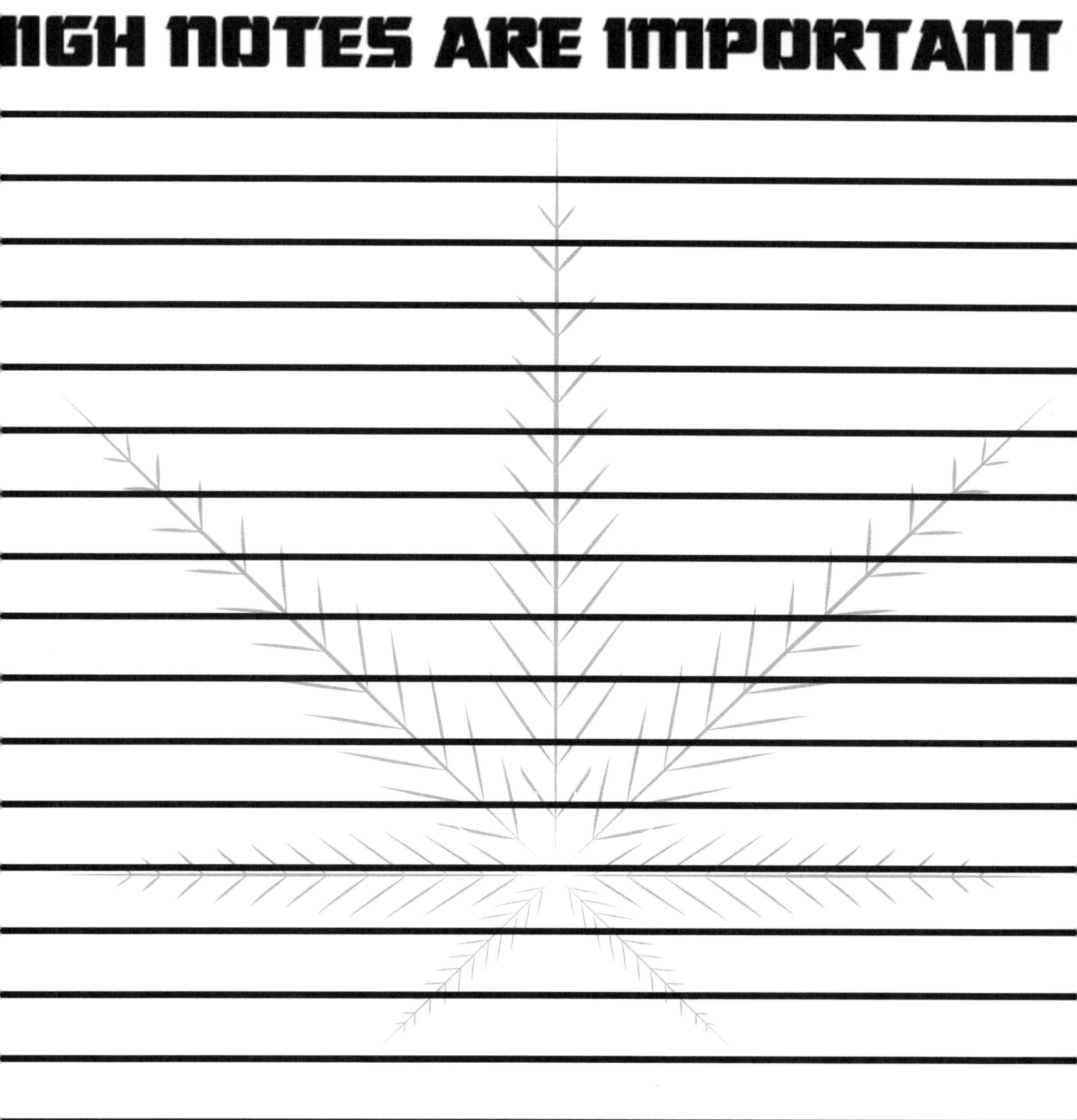

WAYS TO WEED
ANSWER KEY

MUNCHIE MAZE ANSWER KEY

YES WE SMOKE OVER HERE
ANSWER KEY

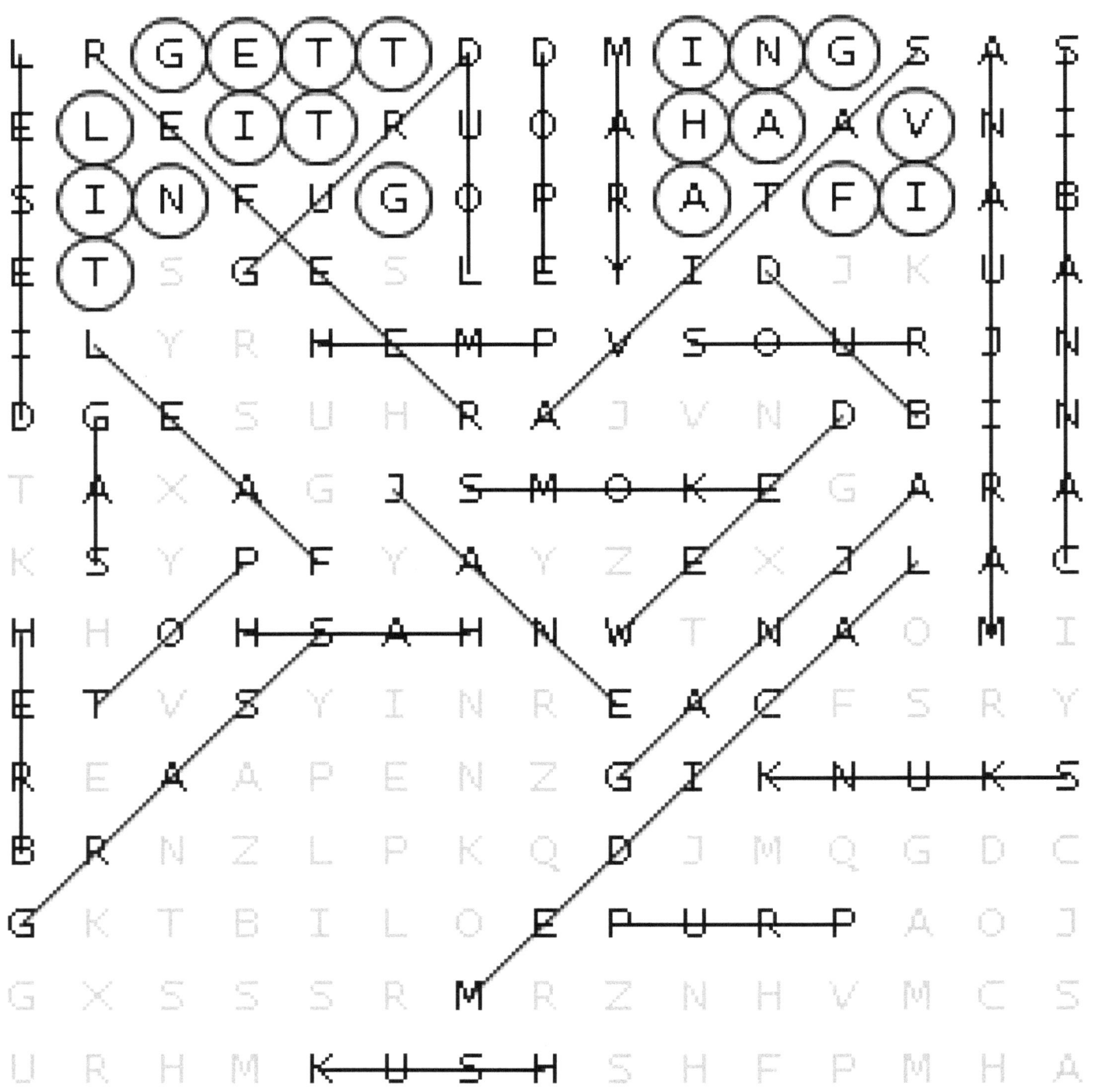

WHEN GETTING HIGH
ANSWER KEY

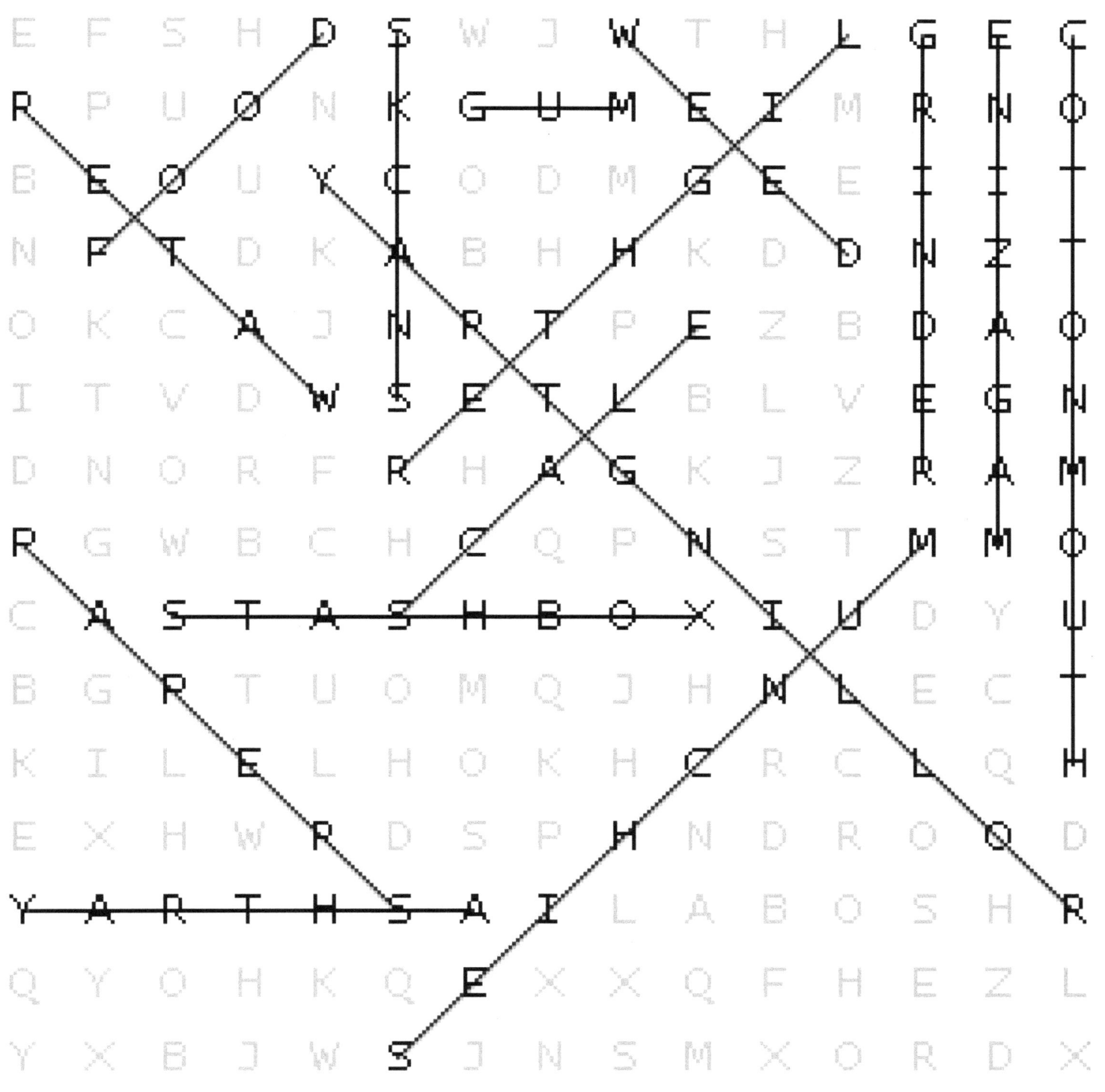

Sudoku Answer Key

3	8	5	2	1	6	7	4	9
1	7	4	3	9	5	6	2	8
9	6	2	8	7	4	3	5	1
7	5	3	9	4	8	1	6	2
6	9	1	7	3	2	5	8	4
2	4	8	6	5	1	9	7	3
8	2	9	1	6	7	4	3	5
4	3	7	5	2	9	8	1	6
5	1	6	4	8	3	2	9	7

Weed Cinema
ANSWER KEY

#		MOVIE TITLE	ACTORS	
1	I	HOW HIGH	Jennifer Aniston & Jason Sudeikis	A
2	K	BEACH BUM	Tommy & Mr. Marin	B
3	M	JAY & SILENT BOB	DeRay Davis & Lil Duval	C
4	A	WE'RE THE MILLERS	Adrien Brody & Matt Bush	D
5	P	FRIDAY	John Cho & Kal Penn	E
6	H	HALF BAKED	Sacha Baron Cohen & Emilio Rivera	F
7	B	CHEECH & CHONG	Matthew McConaughey & Charlie Hunnam	G
8	N	PINEAPPLE EXPRESS	Dave Chapelle & Jim Breuer	H
9	D	HIGH SCHOOL	Method Man & Redman	I
10	C	GROW HOUSE	Jeff Bridges & John Goodman	J
11	R	THE WASH	Matthew McConaughey & Isla Fisher	K
12	F	ALI G IN DA HOUSE	Ashton Kutcher & Seann William Scott	L
13	Q	THIS IS THE END	Jason Mewes & Kevin Smith	M
14	E	HAROLD & KUMAR	Seth Rogers & James Franco	N
15	J	THE BIG LEBOWSKI	Alex Winter & Keanu Reeves	O
16	G	THE GENTLEMEN	Ice Cube & Chris Tucker	P
17	O	DUDE, WHERE'S MY CAR	Seth Rogers & Jonah Hill	Q
18	L	BILL & TED'S EXCELLENT ADVENTURE	Dr. Dre & Snoop Dogg	R

© Published in 2021.
No part of this production may be reproduced, stored in a retrieval system, or transmitted in any form or by any means, electronic, mechanical, photocopying, recording, or otherwise, without the prior permission of the publishers.

www.ingramcontent.com/pod-product-compliance
Lightning Source LLC
Chambersburg PA
CBHW061800290426
44109CB00030B/2901